What Happens If the OZONE Disappears?

Mary Colson

Smart Apple Media

Published by Smart Apple Media, an imprint of Black Rabbit Books
P.O. Box 3263, Mankato, Minnesota 56002
www.smartapplemedia.com

Published by arrangement with Wayland Books, London.

Cataloging-in-Publication Data is available from the Library of Congress
ISBN: 978-1-62588-161-8   (library binding)
ISBN: 978-1-62588-570-8   (eBook)

Picture acknowledgements
NASA: 22, NASA Goddard Space Flight Center 6, STEREO science
team 9 b/g; NOAA: 11; Shutterstock: Achimdiver 23, Africa Studio 24,
AlinaMD 6-7, 26, balounm 3, 26-27, Natalia Bratslavsky 14-15, Tony
Campbell 18-19, deb22 22–23, Eastimages 12, Dirk Ercken 21tl, Mandy
Godbehear 5, guentermanaus 16-17, Chris Gunby 20-21, Angela Harburn
28-29, holbox 13, Debra James 22, Nickolay Khoroshkov 8, emin kuliyev
24-25, Nataiki 28, nmedia 18, Federico Rostagno 10-11, spirit of america
12-13, Michel Stevelmans 17, Zhabska Tetyana 7, wellphoto 9t, Shane
White 14br, worker 4, Wutthichai 19t, gary yim 21tr.

Printed in the United States by CG Book Printers
North Mankato, Minnesota

PO 1770
12-2015

Contents

Protecting Planet Earth

Have you ever wondered what is up there in our atmosphere? On a hot day, do you think about the Sun's rays and protect your skin from burning by using Sun Protection Factor (SPF) lotion? How is it that we don't get burned at other times? Did you know that there's a natural sunblock up there, in the sky, that's under threat?

You cannot see the ozone layer but it is there and it is a vital protective layer for Earth against the Sun's harmful rays.

Climate control

Our planet comes with an in-built SPF called the ozone layer. It was formed millions of years ago and without it, life on Earth as we know it would not exist. The ozone layer is an invisible layer of gas high in the upper atmosphere, on the edge of space. It keeps the climate under control and acts as a filter against the most harmful of the Sun's rays.

Global protection

It is not just human skin that needs protection from the Sun, but every living thing on Earth. From fish in the ocean and **coral reefs** to farmland and crops, and even the ice caps at the North and South Poles, everything depends on the ozone layer. But the ozone layer is under threat. It is at risk of disappearing. What is causing this? And can it be reversed?

Fragile layer

Natural processes on Earth are often interlinked. When something happens, such as the ozone layer thinning or even disappearing, it can trigger a series of actions that can have devastating effects. This book looks at the causes and effects of ozone damage. What will happen if the ozone layer disappears?

Without the ozone layer to protect us, sunny beach holidays could be under threat in the future.

Life Support

Think of the Earth as having an invisible blanket all around it, keeping it safe. In the 1980s, scientists began finding clues that this blanket, the ozone layer, was thinning or even vanishing in places. The scientists were alarmed by these "holes" because they did not know what was causing them.

Green and yellow areas indicate the most ozone.

Blue and purple areas indicate the least ozone.

Ozone depletion is at its most extreme at the two poles. At the North Pole, the hole in the ozone layer is larger than the hole over the South Pole (shown here in 2010).

Where is ozone found?

Ozone is a natural gas that is found in two different layers of the atmosphere. One layer, called the **troposphere**, is at the Earth's surface where we live. Ozone released in the troposphere harms life on Earth because it dirties the air and helps make **smog**, which is unhealthy to **inhale**.

The other layer, called the **stratosphere**, begins at around 12 miles (20 km) above the Earth's surface and ends at around 30 miles (50 km) above the Earth's surface. Ozone in the stratosphere protects life on Earth by absorbing some of the Sun's harmful **ultraviolet** (UV) rays.

Stratosphere   30 miles (50 km)

Troposphere   12 miles (20 km)

Ozone in the stratosphere acts as a shield, protecting us from harmful UV rays. The ozone in the troposphere is a pollutant and damages life on Earth.

NUMBER CRUNCHING

Scientists have calculated that a 1 percent depletion in the ozone layer would allow 2 percent more ultraviolet radiation to reach the Earth's surface. In turn, this means that the rates of skin cancer would rise dramatically.

Deadly sunshine

The thinning of the ozone layer allows more UV light to reach the Earth's surface. UV light and **radiation** from the Sun can cause cancer in humans. It can also destroy plants and disrupt life cycles. It is extremely powerful and can change the whole balance of life on our planet.

The Science of CFCs

The ozone layer, as we have seen, is quite fragile. Without it, we could not live as we do. Scientists have pinpointed the substances that cause the most damage to the ozone layer and it seems that human activity is to blame. Some of the most harmful chemicals that damage the ozone and create the "holes" are the waste products of factory industries.

What are chlorofluorocarbons?

Chlorofluorocarbons

Chlorofluorocarbons (CFCs) are chemical compounds made up of chlorine, fluoride, and carbon. Together, they make a terrible trio that causes ozone destruction.

UV + CFCs = ozone destruction

CFC molecules are heavier than air, so they hang around for a long time and cause a lot of ozone damage. Eventually, over two to five years, they are carried up into the stratosphere by strong winds. Here, UV radiation breaks them apart, releasing the chlorine atoms from the fluoride and carbon atoms. Chlorine is poisonous to humans and deadly to ozone, too. The chlorine reacts with the ozone gases and quickly destroys them, causing a thinning of the protective ozone layer.

Factories churn out smoke containing tons of chemicals. These chemicals are carried up into the atmosphere, where they cause damage to the ozone layer.

CFCs at home

CFCs are used in fridges, freezers, and air-conditioning systems as **coolants**. Some soaps and foams also contain CFCs. Fridges do not harm the ozone when they are working properly, but when they are old and are thrown away, the problems begin. If the cooling system is broken or damaged, CFCs are released into the air and make their way up into the stratosphere.

It is possible to dispose of old fridges and freezers safely by draining the cooling systems of CFCs. These old fridges have been dumped illegally and could leak CFCs into the atmosphere.

The ozone layer is the Earth's main defense against the Sun's harmful rays.

What happens next?

⚠ Just one atom of chlorine can destroy more than 100,000 ozone molecules. In the United States, CFCs are banned. However, in rapidly developing nations such as India, China, and Brazil, there are no laws banning CFCs. This creates the risk that more of the ozone layer will be destroyed.

Pollutants and Poisons

CFCs are not the only pollutants that are damaging the ozone layer: it is under attack from other chemicals, too.

What damages the ozone layer?

Toxic sprays

All over the world, farmers spray **pesticides** on their crops to kill bugs. This improves harvests and means that there is enough food for us to eat. However, these pesticides contain ozone-harming chemicals such as methyl bromide. As methyl bromide is broken apart in the atmosphere, bromine atoms are released. Bromine is 60 times more destructive to ozone than chlorine. So, what might be good for us on the surface of the planet is a disaster for the ozone layer 6 to 12 miles (10 to 20 km) above our heads.

Large-scale agricultural pesticide spraying uses chemicals that help to kill pests, but they also damage the ozone layer.

What are halons?

From fire extinguishers to glues, many products contain halons. Halons, like CFCs and bromine, are harmful to the ozone layer. An ozone-depleting substance is anything that attacks or harms the ozone layer, such as pesticides and halons.

Measuring ozone pollution

Ozone scientists work out how many CFCs and other pollutants are in the stratosphere. They use special balloons with measuring equipment attached to them. They gather stratosphere gas samples and then analyze what gases are there and in what quantities. Sometimes, the scientists go up in aircraft to take samples themselves.

These scientists are launching test balloons in Antarctica. Ozone levels are measured at the North and South Poles because this is where ozone depletion is most extreme.

What happens next?

⚠ In 1987 in Montreal, Canada, 197 countries agreed to phase out CFCs and other chemicals harmful to the ozone layer. If all the countries stick to the agreement, known as the Montreal Protocol, scientists think that the ozone layer will recover by 2100. The problem is that not everyone is meeting the targets set, and all of the time the ozone layer is getting thinner, and our planet is getting hotter...

The Big Burn: 2050

It is 2050 and the world is a very different place from the one we once knew. Targets set by the Montreal Protocol have not been met. The ozone layer was officially destroyed at 8:47 p.m. on March 15, 2040. For a decade, people have been chasing any shade they can find as the unprotected Earth burns in the sunshine. With no ozone and no protection from the Sun's harsh UV light rays, daily life has changed dramatically.

People are forced to live in air-conditioned buildings like this one.

WHERE WILL YOU BE IN 2050? IT'S YOUR FUTURE!

People wear protective anti-UV suits when they go outside.

Biomes (atmosphere-controlled greenhouses), like this one in Arizona, are dotted all over the planet. They are the only way that the human race can survive.

NEWS HEADLINES

Many people now live in **biomes** or bubble houses as they are called. Mirror panels on the walls and roof reflect the Sun's rays in a bid to keep the house cool. Without them, homes would be unbearably hot.

Solar panels are on nearly every roof to harness energy from the Sun and turn it into electricity.

Inside, the oxygen levels and air conditioning are controlled by computers.

Houses do not have gardens anymore. There are no flowers or grass, just dull, dry, dusty earth.

Children do not play out unless they are wearing their reflective sunsuits.

Cases of skin cancer have rocketed.

Sunlight safety hours are enforced. No one is allowed outside between 12 and 4 p.m. Police officers wear full anti-UV suits as they patrol the streets.

Ozone Around the World

One of the main functions of the ozone layer is to stop too much UV light from the Sun from entering our atmosphere. We know this is key to preventing skin cancer and damage to our eyesight. The layer of ozone acts like a giant filter. But why is it thinning in some places more than others, and how does this affect different areas of the world? What are the consequences for the people on Earth?

The ozone layer helps to filter harmful UV light from the Sun. With less ozone to protect us, the Sun's rays are more harmful. Sunburn causes serious damage to human skin.

Where is the ozone layer thinning?

A global issue

All around the world, from Australia and Africa, to China and the United States, there is evidence of ozone depletion. Scientists have found that the thinning of the ozone layer is worst at both poles, which means that more UV is getting through and melting the ice caps. This has consequences in terms of climate change and for rising sea levels which will flood low-lying land.

Ozone thinning is also occurring over the United States and other developed countries that use a lot of ozone-depleting chemicals. A vanishing of the hole directly over a large population would have consequences for human health and for farming.

Everything in moderation

If too much UV light reaches the soil, it kills off bacteria and this makes the soil infertile. People in the United States and Europe rely on the great plains of the U.S. for wheat. If the soil there becomes infertile, wheat prices will rocket and people may go hungry. If the soil in other regions starts to fail, the result would be worldwide **famine**.

NUMBER CRUNCHING

In 2012, the wheat harvest in North America was affected by devastating drought. As a result the price of wheat shot up. The UK imports most of its wheat from the United States. The impact of all this was loaves of bread cost 30 percent more than normal. All food could become more expensive as the climate changes.

Heating up

Perhaps the most serious consequence of more UV radiation is that it causes **global warming**. That could have the biggest consequence of all...

The decrease in soil fertility worldwide is a huge problem for farmers and food producers.

15

The Greenhouse Effect

For millions of years all over the world, humans, plants, and animals have adapted to different temperatures and weather conditions. Over the last century, scientists have noticed that the polar ice caps are melting and the Earth is slowly warming up.

Why is the Earth heating up?

Harm from humans

Since the beginning of the Industrial Revolution in the 19th century, the large-scale burning of fossil fuels such as coal, oil, and natural gas has contributed to the increase in carbon dioxide in the atmosphere. In the 21st century, rapidly developing nations such as China and India need huge quantities of energy, so they burn enormous amounts of coal. On top of this, the burning and clearing of rain forests all over the world billows huge amounts of carbon dioxide into the atmosphere. But what is the problem with this? And why is carbon dioxide called a **greenhouse gas**?

By destroying rain forests, we are sending millions of tons of polluting carbon dioxide up into the atmosphere.

Natural heat

Greenhouse gases, such as carbon dioxide and methane, allow radiation from the Sun to pass through the ozone layer and heat the Earth. This is like the panes of glass in a greenhouse that allow the Sun to heat the interior. Without greenhouse gases, the Earth's surface would on average be about 60° Fahrenheit (33° C) colder. When they are in balance with other gases, they do not cause a problem, but when more greenhouse gases are pumped into the atmosphere, it causes an imbalance.

Global warming

The more greenhouse gases in our atmosphere and the less ozone layer there is, the more radiation is trapped and the planet becomes hotter. The main greenhouse gas is carbon dioxide. According to the Intergovernmental Panel on Climate Change, carbon dioxide makes up about 25 percent of greenhouse gases. It is vital to reduce the amount of carbon dioxide we create.

Industrialized countries have a huge demand for oil. As oil is burned, it emits carbon dioxide and other ozone-harming chemicals.

What happens next?

⚠️ Already, the world is experiencing more extreme weather conditions, and many scientists think the climate is changing. Human actions are to blame so we need to be mindful of our **carbon footprint**; that is, how much carbon dioxide each of us produces through heating our houses, traveling, and daily energy use.

Water Wars: 2100

It is the year 2100. The ozone layer has been destroyed and the planet's climate has been dramatically affected. It is 5.4° Fahrenheit (3° C) hotter on average than ever before. The ice caps have melted and, without the ozone shield, heat from the Sun is causing mass evaporation of the Earth's freshwater supplies. World peace is threatened by the need to survive…

The land is barren and infertile, meaning food shortages for millions.

WHERE WILL YOUR KIDS BE IN 2100? IT'S THEIR FUTURE!

Extreme weather batters many parts of the world and people are forced to leave their homes.

As freshwater supplies dwindle, the whole **food chain** begins to crumble.

NEWS HEADLINES

The rise in sea levels has permanently flooded low-lying countries such as the Netherlands and Bangladesh.

....

Millions of people have moved inland to live, causing mass overcrowding and unrest.

....

Farmland has dried up and farmers struggle to grow crops, leading to crippling food shortages and sky-high prices.

....

Oxygen levels and temperatures in the oceans are changing with the rise in global temperatures. Sea animals cannot adapt quickly enough and many species such as the Atlantic white marlin and the sea otter face extinction.

....

Freshwater supplies are starting to run out, and desperate nations wage war on others in a bid to control this precious resource.

....

Disrupted Life Cycles

Biodiversity is the range and variety of all living things on Earth. With less or no ozone and a hotter Earth, the life cycles of plants will change. This will disrupt the food chain and have a massive impact on human life.

What will no ozone mean for life on Earth?

Too much UV light

If too much UV light reaches the Earth's surface, it will kill bacteria in the soil. This will make the soil less fertile and plants will not grow as well. Artificial fertilizers will only be partially effective. We will not be able to produce enough food for the growing world population, meaning there will be famine and rocketing food prices.

If the soil does not bind together, crops will fail to grow and many parts of the world will become **dust bowls**. This will cause massive breathing problems for millions of people all over the world.

Desertification is a huge problem in some parts of the world. The soil becomes poor and the lack of rain means that it cannot bind together, creating dangerous dust bowls.

Soil **erosion** is already an issue in parts of Africa as a result of overgrazing. Unless this trend is reversed, the soil will become so poor that nothing will grow there.

Ecosystems destroyed

The **ecosystems** of forests and deserts will be harmed by increased heat and less ozone. The rise in temperatures will cause mass extinction of animals and plant species, possibly even a million in total. Humans and animals will have to move to coastal areas in order to survive. This will result in overcrowding and increased competition for already limited resources.

NUMBER CRUNCHING

The International Union for the Conservation of Nature calculates that humans are driving thousands of species of plants and animals to extinction. For the first time in history, species are dying out quicker than new ones can evolve. If this trend continues, our food chain will be massively affected and food shortages could become a common event.

Ozone and Oceans

With a thinning in the ozone layer and an increase in the UV radiation getting through to the planet's surface, there is a marked effect on marine life. Many species are dying out, most importantly, algae, corals, and crustaceans like crabs.

How is ocean life at risk?

Coral bleaching is becoming a major problem in the Great Barrier Reef due to an increase in ocean temperatures.

Great Barrier Reef at risk

The largest living organism on Earth is Australia's Great Barrier Reef. It is a 1,600-mile-long (2,600 km) system of plants and islands made up of nearly 3,000 separate reefs. More than a million different animal species live on the reef including millions of corals. Corals are animals and are very sensitive to UV light and temperature changes.

Krill is a tiny creature at the bottom of the ocean food chain. It does not reproduce as well in warmer waters. If there is even a 1 degree rise in ocean temperature, there will not be enough krill for animals such as penguins and seals to eat. In turn, this will cause food shortages for larger predators such as sharks and whales. With a collapse of the food chain, sea animals will die out.

The UV killer

Scientists have been monitoring the bleaching effect of high UV radiation on the corals and are alarmed at the rate at which they are dying. Like all plants, coral needs some UV light to make food through a process called **photosynthesis**. Too much UV light, however, stops photosynthesis happening. The plants turn white, or bleach, and the coral becomes at risk of dying.

Salty water

With a hotter Earth comes more evaporation. This will cause the sea to get saltier and fish to die. Even now in the Persian Gulf, rising salt levels are causing the already rare dugong to become endangered.

The endangered dugong is native to the Persian Gulf. With a change in salt levels in the water, the seagrass the dugong feeds on is dying, so the creature is at risk of becoming extinct.

New Worlds: 2200

It is 2200. The Earth has changed and human life has become harder to sustain. With no ozone layer, rising ocean levels, and a 18° Fahrenheit (10° C) rise in average temperatures, disease is everywhere and malaria and cancer have wiped out billions. Those left are struggling to cope with heat waves that last for months on end.

With fewer crops able to be grown, food has been replaced by pills containing life-supporting vitamins and minerals.

NEWS HEADLINES

People now take meal pills to survive.

The areas around the Equator and the Tropics are barren wastelands; the **parched** lands are uninhabitable for humans.

Mass **migration** to the cooler Northern Hemisphere has put even more pressure on resources.

The ocean now covers 80 percent of the Earth's surface.

Once great cities, such as London, New York, Sydney, and Rio have vanished underwater.

Governments struggle to agree on the best way to divide up the planet's remaining resources.

The first space shuttle carrying humans to Mars has set off. It is hoped that they will be able to establish a settlement there.

The ice caps have melted, flooding some cities and completely drowning others.

Are There Alternatives to Ozone?

As the ozone layer is being depleted, what can be done to stop this process and is there an alternative to ozone?

Can we create new supplies of ozone?

Solar energy

It is possible to create ozone in science laboratories but it cannot be made where it is needed or in the gigantic quantities required. Ozone is produced naturally when sunlight shines on air. It is made by several oxygen molecules reacting with each other in a chemical reaction. But this happens only in sunlight. It is why there is more ozone in summer and the "hole" seems to close. However, if it is nighttime, cloudy, or winter, ozone won't be produced.

If we continue to pollute and send ozone-depleting substances into the atmosphere, the ozone will certainly disappear even faster.

The Sun makes life on Earth possible but the harmful effects of its rays can be prevented only by the ozone layer.

The Sun provides the huge amounts of energy for the production of natural ozone in the ozone layer. Scientists at the United States Environmental Protection Agency estimate that to artificially produce the amount of ozone normally in the ozone layer, it would take double the total annual amount of electricity that is currently produced in the United States. In other words, it would be an impossible task.

Beyond repair?

Remember that the key reason that the ozone layer is being depleted is that chemicals such as CFCs destroy ozone. If the destruction of ozone is occurring faster than the making of naturally occurring ozone, there will be a gradual depletion of this fragile protective layer. Eventually, whether it is sunny or not, the destruction will be more than the new ozone can repair and we will be left with a permanently damaged ozone layer.

What Does the Future Hold?

No one knows for sure what the future holds for the ozone layer. Some scientists believe the hole will not get any bigger, but others fear that it will get much worse with more developing nations using CFCs.

When will the ozone layer no longer be at risk?

Predicting the damage

Due to international bans on chemicals such as CFCs, the rate at which the ozone layer is disappearing is slowing down. The problem is that ozone-eating chemicals such as CFCs take about 50 years to reach the ozone layer. They then stay there and destroy it for much longer. The full extent of the damage will not be known for at least half a century or more after the last CFCs and other ozone pollutants are released.

It is hard to predict the Earth's future climate, but with ozone depletion and global warming, more extreme weather is almost certain.

Ozone Day

In 1994, the **United Nations** declared that every year, September 16 would become the "International Day for the Preservation of the Ozone Layer." On this day, special events are held to raise awareness of the problem of ozone depletion.

What happens next?

⚠ Our decisions and actions can make a difference and can change the world. At home, turning down the heating, avoiding CFC sprays, walking rather than driving, and using public transport are all ways you can minimize your own carbon footprint. This will help to keep the greenhouse effect under control and make the ozone layer safe.

⚠ You could join a campaign group and help to raise awareness of the threat to the ozone layer from our activities on Earth.

⚠ All these are ways you can do your bit and be a great guardian of the planet for future generations.

Glossary

biomes climate-controlled buildings like a greenhouse

carbon footprint the amount of carbon dioxide we produce in our daily lives

coolants chemicals that prevent a machine or engine from overheating

coral bleaching when corals get too much UV light and turn white

coral reefs ridges of coral built by billions of tiny shellfish called coral polyps

desertification process by which land loses its water content and becomes increasingly dry and infertile

dust bowls areas where vegetation has been lost and soil eroded, usually as a result of drought or poor farming methods

ecosystems plants, animals, and the environments they inhabit together

erosion the process of eroding by wind, water, or other natural processes

evaporation process by which water is heated up by the Sun and turned into vapor

famine extreme shortage of food

food chain order in which animals feed on other plants and animals; for example, a smaller animal will be eaten by a larger one

global warming increase in the world's temperatures

greenhouse gases gases in the atmosphere, particularly carbon dioxide and methane, which trap the Sun's heat and so cause global warming

inhale to breathe in

krill very tiny shellfish, like microscopic shrimp

migration moving from one country to another

parched extremely dry

pesticides chemicals used to kill pests such as insects

photosynthesis process by which plants change carbon dioxide and water into food using energy from the Sun

radiation energy from sunlight, which can be very harmful

smog a polluting cloud of smoke and fog

stratosphere region of atmosphere from 12 to 30 miles (20 to 50 km) above the Earth's surface

troposphere lowest layer of the atmosphere, from the ground to 12 miles (20 km) above the Earth's surface

ultraviolet harmful light waves from the Sun

United Nations an organization formed in 1945 to promote international peace and security

Further Information

Books

Climate Change: Can the Earth Cope? Richard Spilsbury, Wayland 2012.

Eco Alert: Climate Change, Rebecca Hunter, Franklin Watts, 2012.

Ecosystems: Climate Change, Peter Benoit, Children's Press, 2011.

Unstable Earth: What Happens If the Rain Forests Disappear?
Mary Colson, Smart Apple Media, 2015.

Unstable Earth: What Happens If We Overfish the Oceans?
Angela Royston, Smart Apple Media, 2015.

Unstable Earth: What Happens When an Ice Cap Melts?
Angela Royston, Smart Apple Media, 2015.

Websites

www.earthday.org
If you would like to play a part in Earth Day every April, visit this
website to learn more.

www.epa.gov/climatechange/kids/impacts/signs/index.html
stThe U.S. Environmental Protection Agency's website for kids shows the
effects of shrinking sea ice, melting glaciers, rising sea levels and much
more.

http://www.epa.gov/sunwise/kids/index.html
stVisit this U.S. Environmental Protection Agency's website to learn how
the ozone layer and sunlight affect you each and every day.

www.kidsforsavingearth.org
Check out this fun website for some great information about our precious
planet and ideas and activities to help you make a difference.

Index